Dear Parent:
Your child's love of reading starts here!

Every child learns to read in a different way and at his or her own speed. Some go back and forth between reading levels and read favorite books again and again. Others read through each level in order. You can help your young reader improve and become more confident by encouraging his or her own interests and abilities. From books your child reads with you to the first books he or she reads alone, there are I Can Read Books for every stage of reading:

SHARED READING
Basic language, word repetition, and whimsical illustrations, ideal for sharing with your emergent reader

BEGINNING READING
Short sentences, familiar words, and simple concepts for children eager to read on their own

READING WITH HELP
Engaging stories, longer sentences, and language play for developing readers

READING ALONE
Complex plots, challenging vocabulary, and high-interest topics for the independent reader

ADVANCED READING
Short paragraphs, chapters, and exciting themes for the perfect bridge to chapter books

I Can Read Books have introduced children to the joy of reading since 1957. Featuring award-winning authors and illustrators and a fabulous cast of beloved characters, I Can Read Books set the standard for beginning readers.

A lifetime of discovery begins with the magical words **"I Can Read!"**

Visit www.icanread.com for information
on enriching your child's reading experience.

For Rev. Paul and Christina Jeanes,
who give everyone a break!
—H. P.

To all kids and grown-ups who have had to
search for a breakaway hamster! —L. A.

Gouache and black pencil were used to prepare the full-color art.

I Can Read Book® is a trademark of HarperCollins Publishers.

Amelia Bedelia is a registered trademark of Peppermint Partners, LLC.

Amelia Bedelia Gets a Break. Text copyright © 2018 by Herman S. Parish III. Illustrations copyright © 2018 by Lynne Avril. All rights reserved. No part of this book may be used or reproduced in any manner whatsoever without written permission except in the case of brief quotations embodied in critical articles and reviews. Manufactured in China. For information address HarperCollins Children's Books, a division of HarperCollins Publishers, 195 Broadway, New York, NY 10007. www.icanread.com

Library of Congress Control Number: 2018931147

ISBN 978-0-06-265889-0 (hardback)—ISBN 978-0-06-265888-3 (pbk. ed.)

18 19 20 21 22 SCP 10 9 8 7 6 5 4 3 2 1 First Edition

Greenwillow Books

I Can Read!

1
BEGINNING READING

Amelia Bedelia
· Gets a Break ·

by **Herman Parish** ✿ pictures by **Lynne Avril**

Greenwillow Books, *An Imprint of* HarperCollins*Publishers*

Harry's HOUSE

Amelia Bedelia was taking care of
the class pet over school break.
Harry the hamster was here!
She moved her dollhouse aside
to make room for his habitat.

Amelia Bedelia loved her dollhouse.
She sometimes wished she was
small enough to live in it.

That night, Amelia Bedelia

snuggled under her covers.

She heard Harry squeak.

"Good night, Harry," said Amelia Bedelia.

She liked having a pet project.

In the morning, Amelia Bedelia

let Harry sleep in.

She made breakfast for him.

Dawn and Clay stopped by.

"We miss Harry," said Dawn.

"You can help me feed him,"

said Amelia Bedelia.

"Where is Harry?" asked Dawn.

"Still sleeping," said Amelia Bedelia.

"Are you sure?" said Clay.

"His house looks empty to me."

12

"Harry must have broken out," said Dawn.

"I did not see a rash," said Amelia Bedelia.

"Harry made a break for it," said Clay.

"He escaped. Vanished. Harry is gone," said Dawn.

Amelia Bedelia's lower lip trembled. She wanted to break into tears.

"It is not your fault," said Dawn.

"Hamsters are brave and curious," said Clay.

"When my cat was lost, I made posters.

My neighbors saw them

and brought her back," said Dawn.

The three friends got to work.

Amelia Bedelia felt better.

It felt good just to do something.

The posters also made her remember

Harry's tiny ears and bright eyes.

She missed his whiskers most of all.

"We should call him
Harry Houdini," said Clay.

"Who?" asked Amelia Bedelia.

"Houdini," said Clay.

"He was a famous magician," said Dawn.

"He could escape from anyplace."

"I am learning some magic tricks
over the break,"
said Clay.

"Let's offer a reward," said Dawn.

"I am broke," said Clay.

"You look fine to me," said Amelia Bedelia.

"What part of you is broken?"

"I mean, I do not have any money,"

said Clay.

Clay nibbled a carrot.

"Hey, hands off," said Dawn.

"That treat is for Harry."

"I am a magician," said Clay.

"I am making this carrot disappear."

"Please make Harry appear,"

said Amelia Bedelia.

"Harry may be gone for good,"
said Clay.

"There is nothing good about that,"
said Amelia Bedelia.

"He must be close by," said Dawn.

"Let's keep looking."

"Why did Harry run away?" asked Clay.

"He has lots of cool stuff in his habitat.

I want to run on his wheel."

"Do a magic spell and shrink yourself,"
said Dawn. "Then find Harry."

That is when an idea popped
into Amelia Bedelia's head.
She tiptoed to her dollhouse.
She peeked inside.

Harry was asleep on the bed.

Amelia Bedelia felt like cheering.

Then she remembered that hamsters

stay awake at night and sleep all day.

"Shhh! Come over here! Look!"

said Amelia Bedelia.

Clay, Dawn, and Amelia Bedelia

watched Harry snooze.

"Who is next to him?" said Dawn.

Clay was counting. ". . . four, five, six!
I see six babies. Harry is a father!"

"No. Harry is a mother," said Dawn.

"Harry needs a new name,"
said Amelia Bedelia.

"A new name for a new mom,"
said Dawn.

Bunny Izzy Sweety Cuddles
Penelope Cookie Pixie Fluffernutter
Daisy Violet Poopsie Zizzie
Nibble Dinky
Lily Butterscotch Rosie Zoey
Ivy Cupcake Lady Ginger
Squeakie Tinkerbell Olivia
Sugar Tilly Honey Goldilocks

They thought and
thought and thought.
Clay snapped his fingers.
"Presto!" he said.
"How about Harriet?"
"Perfect," said Amelia Bedelia.

27

Amelia Bedelia knew exactly
what to do next.

They called Miss Edwards.

They told their teacher the story.

She laughed and laughed.

"Who knew that Harry was really Harriet!" said Amelia Bedelia.

"Sounds like our class pet pulled the wool over our eyes," said Miss Edwards.

"So far, this break has been really fun," said Amelia Bedelia.

"Our class pet got lost, had a family, and got found," said Dawn.

"And got a new name!"

"Shazam!" said Clay.

"This has been our lucky break,"

Amelia Bedelia said to her friends.

"We lost one class pet,

but we found seven!

And we did it all together!"